This book is dedicated to all the
Northern women who share their love
of the fireplace with those that visit
there.

Northern Fireplaces

By

Laura Diamond-c

Not that long ago every
woman was taught when very young,
where to find and gather the special
roots, leaves, flowers, berries and stems
that were needed by the People of the
North for their journey through this
world and to aid their spirits journey
into the next.

Today only a few of the wild
plants are gathered by the women and
fewer still are used in the preparation
of food and fewer still for medicinal
care of her family. In this modern age
of miracle medicines and commercial
cures, healing the family, has not only
fallen out of use but also out of
memory. This is the direct result of
technology on tradition and culture. If
you have a serious illness such as
pneumonia or cancer you would be

foolish to try to doctor yourself, of course, but you would be equally foolish to buy expensive remedies for cut, bruises, simple stomach aches, bee stings, headaches, nervousness or tired blood, when you can find the ingredients growing just outside your fireplace. So I hope you don't scoff at the suggestions for medicinal cures that you find in this book or reject them untried.

Women are the keeper of the keys. The center of all things and as we sit at the fire, life radiates out from all those around us. Early in the morning before the dew burns off is the best time to gather the plants you'll need. It is also the best way to get to know them and learn from them what they are best used for. Take a basket along to fill with your gatherings and also some tobacco to leave as an offering of thanks to Mother Earth for her gift to you. In this hand book I'll teach you to identify and use each of the plants that grow in your area. These Plants have been used for generations by the People of the Southern Territories.

If you look at the plants around your Fireplace you will be able to identify the ones that you can use in your cooking, to heal your body and to add vital minerals and vitamins to nourish the body and the mind. Gathering from the forest is also a very good source of Soul food.

In early spring the forest becomes a beautiful scented place to spend time. The heady scent of wild

rose and clover fills the air around you.
Both of these lovely plants should be
gathered and dried for later use.

Wild Rose

Pick the petals and dry them and keep
them in an air tight container. To
refresh your room, open the lid for an
hour or so. These petals can also be
chewed and placed on stings for
instant relief. The rose hips are
gathered later when they are ripe and
red. These are high in vitamin C and
can be used to make jam or tea. They
are also nice to eat fresh. The seeds can
be easily removed.

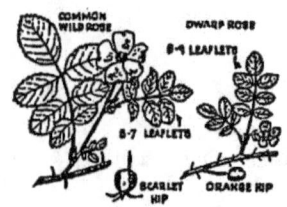

Wild Strawberries

These delicious berries are usually small but are very good. Gather and dry the berries and leaves as they make a tea that's full of vitamins and really nutritious for little children.

Wild Strawberry

Cloudberry

Cloudberry grows close to the ground in moist areas of bog and peat throughout the Territories, and it is one of the first to bloom in the spring. The berry is bright red to start but is ripe and ready to eat when it turns golden. It's better to store the berries in a basket in a dark cool place if you are not going to eat them right away or make them into jam, jelly or pies. The berries can be chewed and applied to sores and wounds and the Cloudberry flower can be made into a tea for sore eyes.

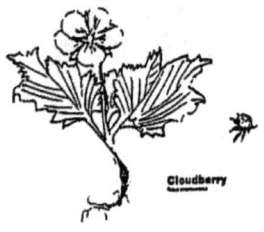

Cloudberry

Wild Mint

Wild Mint grows in meadows and lakes and anywhere that is moist. You can grow Mint in your yard by transplanting the plants or by cuttings. The stem is square and purplish and mauve flowers grow where the leaves are attached to the stem. The leaves are gathered to make Tea or added to other teas to enhance flavor or for the medicinal properties. People drink Mint Tea to sooth their stomachs or calm a cold. The leaves are also used as a room deodorizer and if spread on the floor of the fireplace they give off a delicious mint aroma when walked on.

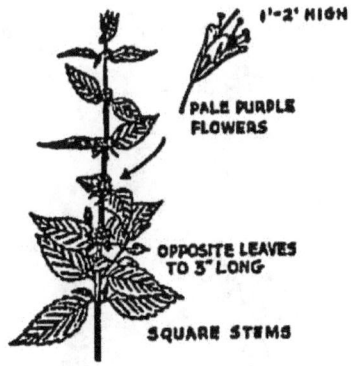

Red Raspberry

Mint Jelly

Make a strong tea of Mint leaves, add pectin and sugar bring to a rolling boil for one minute, and pour into sterilized jars and seal.

Red Raspberry

Raspberries make a nice jam and good snack. Gather the leaves and stems as well when you are out picking because these made into a tea for pregnant women is known and used for generations by the People to make child birth easier.

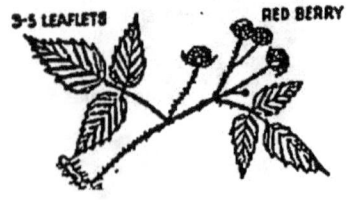

Red Raspberry

Black Current

Black Currents are good to
eat. Early morning is the best time to
gather the leaves and stems. These are
used to make tea and cough syrup in
winter. You will know when they are
ready to pick when you walk through
the woods as the leaves give off a
tomcat odor when they are brushed.

1-2" LONG
CLUSTER OF
WHITISH
FLOWERS

SMOOTH BLACK
BERRIES

Currants

Black Current Sauce

Four cups of berries in a pot
with a little water and sugar boil until
a thick sauce forms. Serve warm over
Bannock or ice cream.

Mountain Cranberry

There are Low bush and
High bush Cranberries. Low bush
Cranberries are small berries that
grow close to the ground like
kinnikinnick or Bear-Berry. It has
leathery, shiny leaves that stay green
all year. The berries are dark red and
shiny. (To tell them apart you will find
that cranberry leaves have black bristly
points on the underside of the leaves

and Kinnikinnick does not.) These berries are high in vitamin C and can be used to make jellies, jams and deserts. Cranberries can be used in medicines for coughs and colds and the juice is a good tonic for your kidneys.

Cranberry

Silverberry

Silverberry is a beautiful pale green shrub that grows mostly along rivers and its yellow flowers are sweetly scented. The twigs have rusty brown scales. Silverberry reproduces

from seeds and sending out runners
from the roots. These berries can be
eaten but they are good to gather for
their long oval seed. The berries are
ready in June and are hard to see as
they also are a pale green. These can be
used as beads to decorate clothing.

Silver Berry or Silver Buffalo Berry

Seeds to Beads

Boil the berries to remove
the flesh. While the seeds are soft
pierce them with a needle and thread.

Let the seeds dry on the thread. Oil the seeds to keep them from drying out and sew them onto clothing.

Soapberry

Soapberry is a shrub that grows over a meter high in open woods and gravelly or sandy areas. The leaves are long and oval with silver hairs on the underside. Twigs and leaves are covered with scales and are rough to the touch. In August the shrub has many ripe red juicy berries. Soapberry is used as a medicine to cure constipation send a tea made from the leaves and stem can be used as a wash for cuts and swellings.

Soap Berry or Buffalo Berry

Now we are going to familiarize you
with plants that grow right outside
your Fireplace.

Plantain

Common Plantain grows as
a weed everywhere people have settled.
The leaves have five to seven obvious
ribs and the stems are 30 cm long with
a dense narrow spike of tiny yellowish
white flowers. These flowers are

replaced by seeds and are good food
for the birds. (Even your house birds)

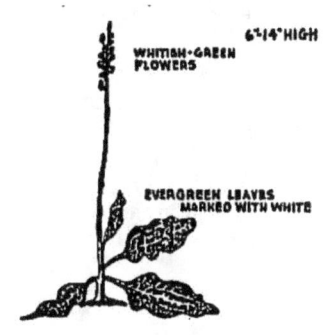

6"-14"HIGH

WHITISH-GREEN
FLOWERS

EVERGREEN LEAVES
MARKED WITH WHITE

PLANTAIN

Plantain Salad

Pick young leaves early in
spring. Mix with other salad greens,
young dandelion shoots and wild
onion. Add tomatoes and cucumber
toss with oil and vinegar.

Plantain has strong healing
powers, so strong that wounds
wrapped with the bruised leaves will
heal quickly. Plantain was thought to

control the path leading directly to the realm of the dead. Plantain is often called white man footsteps because everywhere he walked the plants sprung up.

Common Yarrow

Yarrow grows in dry open areas almost everywhere. It is topped by large flat white flower clusters and each tiny flower is yellow in the center. Yarrow has a tough wooly stem and the leaves look like tiny ferns. Yarrow is collected and hung upside down to dry in a dark dry place for several days. The whole plant is used to make tea for coughs and colds, skin infections, sunburns and insect bites. The flower heads can be made into a tea and drank will stop nose bleeds. Yarrow can also be used to stop a wound from bleeding.

Yarrow has a strong spicy smell and you can use it to keep mosquitoes away by rubbing on your clothing or throwing it into your fire.

8"-20" HIGH

FLAT, WHITE
FLOWER HEAD
2"-4" ACROSS

YARROW

Fireweed

Fireweed grows just about everywhere in recently burnt areas, ditches, roadsides and on the tundra. The flowers are bright pink and grow along the stalk.

All parts of the Fireweed are edible, the leaves can be dried and used for tea and young shoots are good when cooked and can also be used in salad.

When mixed with water and fat, fireweed can be used as a balm for rashes and other skin problems. Fireweed is also loved by the bees and they produce a delicious honey.

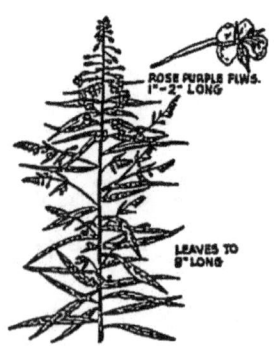

Fireweed

Silverweed

I'm going to mention this lovely plant because it blooms from spring to autumn and makes a lovely plant for your yard or garden. The leaves and flowers when pressed and mounted will keep its color and last for many years. At one time travelers and runners put Silverweed in their shoes to make their journey more comfortable and pleasant.

This lovely plant grows on gravely shores of rivers or lakes. It has green leaves with silvery undersides and long reddish runners that creep along the ground taking root as they go. The yellow flowers have five petals and are shaped like roses. When it's raining the leaves gather together to form a protective roof over the fragile flower.

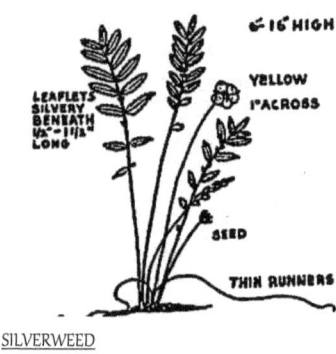

SILVERWEED

Drying Wild Plants

Plants like Yarrow and Indian Paint Brush are easy to preserve by drying. Select some plants and hang them upside down from a line in a dark dry place, like a closet. Leave them for several days till they feel stiff and dry. Put them in a jar or vase and add some wild grass and other dried flowers. These arrangements make nice gifts or brighten up a room. They look real nice in your Fireplace too.

Cat-Tail

Cat-tail grow in many places in the North, they have a distinctive fuzzy tail at the tip of their dense brown spikes. You can eat all parts of the Cat-tail as long as it is growing in a clean, natural marsh:

Young spikes can be eaten like corn in the cob. Young shoots can be eaten as greens. The pollen from the male can be used to make pancakes and muffins. Roots can be pounded into flour. The down or fluff can be used to stuff pillows or babies diapers for an easy to clean liner, helping baby stay dry and warm.

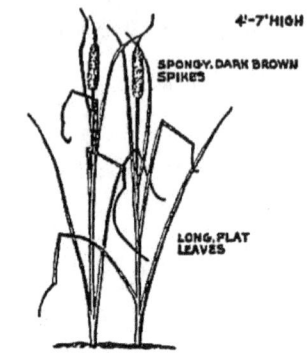

SPONGY, DARK BROWN
SPIKES

4'-7' HIGH

LONG, FLAT
LEAVES

CAT-TAIL

Rat Root

Rat Root grows along streams and in wet areas. It has long sword like leaves with brownish flowers crowded onto a spadix. The root is thick with many small rootlets dangling from it.

Rat Root is one of the most widely known and used medicine and the Northern people use the root for

coughs, colds, sore throats and

stomach problems.

RAT ROOT

Yellow Pond Lily

Yellow pond lily can be
found floating on the surface of ponds
and lakes. They are large heart shaped
leaves surrounding yellow flowers. The
underwater root is attached to the
flower by a long flattened stem. These

roots are harvested in the fall by
wading into the water and uprooting
the plants with your feet or a rake.
Prepare the root by slicing it and
frying it in butter or oil or boil it with
sugar. (Fattening though)

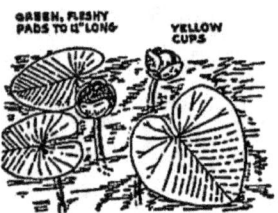

YELLOW POND LILY

Labrador Tea

Labrador Tea is a bush that
has evergreen leaves with wooly
undersides. The young leaves are white
underneath and the older leaves are a
rusty red. Small white flowers grow in
clusters at the top of the plant.

Labrador tea is used as a relaxing drink to make you sleep or cure a headache. You only drink this tea sparingly when you need it as too much is not good for you. Hang this plant in closets to keep moths away.

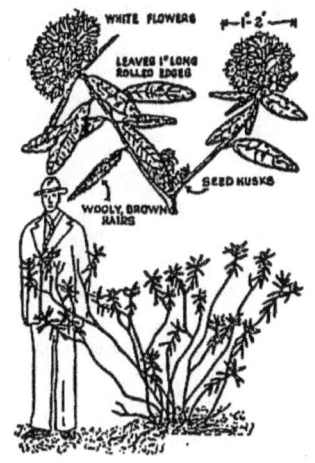

LABRADOR TEA

Make your own Northern Potpourri: Labrador Tea leaves: Strong spicy smell. Rose petals: Sweet delicate smell.

Pine needles and cones: Green woodsy smell. Gather bark and other leaves and petals for a nice looking blend. Dry these for several days. Mix together and put this blend in a jar in your room so you will have the scent of nature all year long. (Spruce boughs make a nicely scented floor covering as does Balsam)

Willow

There are over forty different kinds of willow here and a few are as large as trees but most are low shrubs with branches that stand up or are low to the ground. Willow leaves are long and pointed. Besides being an important food for many animals Willow is used by the people for whistles, pipe stems, bows, canoe ribs, snow shoes, snares and baskets.

Willow bark contains a compound called Salicin from which headache and pain relievers were first made.

Tea from willow bark can be used as a pain reliever. You can boil willow to make dye for clothing too.

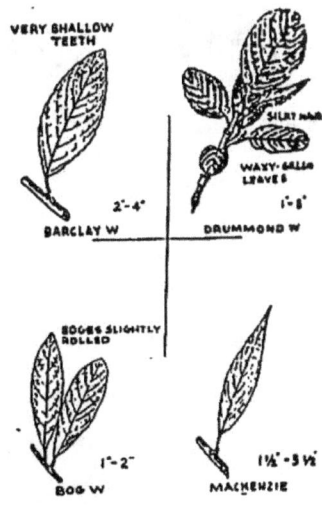

Miscellaneous Willow

NORTHWEST SILVERLEAF COYOTE

Sand bar Willow

Black Spruce

Growing in wet lands and rocky soil
Black Spruce is one of the most
common trees. Its branches bunch up
at the top of the tree but the branches
lower down the trunk tends to droop.
The bark of the trunk is rough and
scaly and the four sided needles are
short and stick out on all sides of the
branch with many pointing upwards.

The cones, boughs, inner bark and gum are used as a medicine by the northern people. It can be used for colds, headaches, toothaches, skin rashes and sore eyes. The boughs are also used for flooring and bedding for camps out on the land.

Black Spruce

Paper Birch

Birch grows in rocky well drained forests and it is easy to spot because of its white papery bark. The Northern people have used Birch for medicine, food, storage or decoration. The bark can be pulled off in strips to be used for making baskets, canoes, snowshoes, toboggans, knife handles, drums, frames and paddles. The bark can be used as a cast for a broken arm or leg. The tree can also be tapped for birch syrup.

CONE SCALE   NUT

Northwest white birch

Alaska Paper Birch

Tamarack

Tamarack grows in wet and boggy areas and in the mountains where there has been landslides. It has scaly bark and long slender branches with soft green needle- like leaves. The inside layer of bark is boiled and used to wash wounds and a tea made from the small fresh branches is especially good for stomach problems.

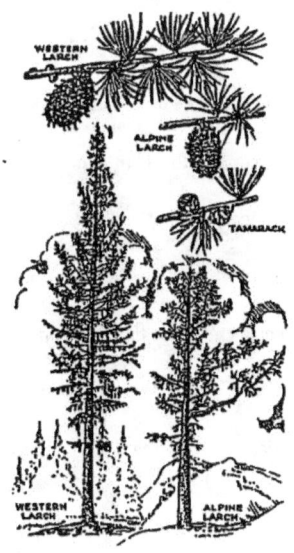

Dandelion Salad

In early spring pick tender dandelion leaves before the flower head appears. Once the flower is growing the dandelion is bitter tasting. Cut the dandelion with a sharp knife just below the soil. Peel off the old leaves and dirt.

Dandelion is an excellent blood cleanser and should be eaten every spring. These young shoots taste very good and can be mixed with other salad ingredients. Dandelion root can be washed free of soil, chopped fine and roasted until dark brown and used as a chocolaty flavored coffee substitute. Dandelion coffee is very beneficial to your health.

Notes:

Notes: